THE
GREEK ANTHOLOGY

SELECTIONS FROM

THE
Greek Anthology

Translated by
ANDREW SINCLAIR

THE MACMILLAN COMPANY
NEW YORK

Library of Congress Catalog Card Number: 68-10248

First American Edition

THE MACMILLAN COMPANY, NEW YORK

Printed in the United States of America

to Marianne

CONTENTS

THE WRITERS OF THE GREEK ANTHOLOGY

SECOND CENTURY AD

FOURTH CENTURY AD

FIFTH CENTURY AD

SIXTH CENTURY AD

TENTH CENTURY AD

WRITERS OF UNKNOWN DATE

ANONYMOUS EPIGRAMS

EPIGRAMS ON THE FAMOUS DEAD

PREFACE

The Greek Anthology is a collection of more than four thousand epigrams, the bulk of which were written between the sixth century BC and the sixth century AD. Thus the Anthology spans Greek history from the rise of the city-state in Greece itself, through the Persian and Peloponnesian Wars, through the conquests of Alexander of Macedon, through the flourishing Hellenic civilization of Alexandria, through the Roman Empire when the Greeks were the teachers of their masters, and through the barbarian invasions and the rise of Christianity until the reign of Justinian allowed in Byzantium the last flowering of Greek art and letters.

The Anthology is a chronicle of these changes. The stern epigrams of Simonides praise the virtues of an honourable death in war, virtues necessary to a military state such as early Athens. But by the time of Plato, the city-state has declined in power. The epigrams now speak of love and drink and work and poverty. If death is the subject, it is a personal tragedy, the death of one man or woman rather than the death of the three hundred

Spartans at Thermopylae. The epigrams now point to the pleasure and pain of the individual life.

This tradition is carried on by the Alexandrian school, although the epigrams, except for those of Callimachus, decline in quality, as the age of gold becomes a silver age. There is more polish in the style and less bite, more nicety in the content and less feeling. And, by the time of Roman dominance, the epigrams are often little more than *bons mots* for feasts. Lucilius and his imitators want to raise a belly-laugh, not a twist of the gut.

With the barbarian invasions and the coming of Christianity, however, a mood of despair overtakes the last of the urban pagans. Palladas looks round Alexandria and the Mediterranean world, and he is sickened by the sight. Civilization is doomed, either at the hands of Vandals or monks. Palladas wants to die. There is no hope. As his contemporary Glycon writes:

> All is dust and all is laughter,
>   All is trivial.
> Chaos before and chaos after,
>   Unreason hatches all.

Yet the Anthology does not end here. Justinian makes Byzantium the centre of an empire. Round him cluster scholars and administrators, proud of this last and greatest of the city-states. A group of officials, Prefects and Consuls and civil servants, write the last important poems in the Anthology, nearly as good in quality as those written a thousand years before.

The last epigram selected in this version of the Anthology is written by an anthologist, Constantinus Cephalas, one of those monks whom Palladas despised. Two other monks in the fourteenth century, Planudes and the unknown author of the Palatine Manuscript, preserved the Anthology for the modern reader.

The epigrams of the Anthology contain a revealing picture of Greek social life and thought. The poverty of Greek society and its dependence on the land is continually stressed. Beggary is the usual fate of those too old to work. In one of the epigrams, an old fisherman hangs up his nets for the last time as a gift to the God of the Sea. Then Macedonius the Consul makes him say: 'Now I am in evil old age, Poverty, from which there is no escape, is young and lusty.' Few Greeks were ever free from the fear of lacking the simple things of life.

Similarly, death is a recurrent theme in the epigrams. The background of Greek religion was based on common ideas about the dead, that they should be honoured and could help the living. The state religion of the cities praised those patriots who had died for their city and those Gods who protected the virtues of the good citizen. Yet death itself was usually faced either in terror or resignation, especially when the decline of the city-state had dragged state religion down into a peasant belief in little local gods to be bribed with petty offerings. Callimachus shows this Greek acceptance of annihilation by a conversation between a living man and a dead man, Charidas:

Q. Charidas, what is below?
A. Great darkness.
Q. What about resurrection?
A. A lie.

Q. And the God of the Dead?
A. A myth. We perish utterly.

If poverty and death were the two chief fears of the Greeks, it was because their society never discovered how to avoid the disasters of nature, famine, earthquake, storm and drought. The Greeks had little love of nature; they were too conscious of its harshness. Yet they trusted the land, although its very poverty drove them to trade on the sea. The epigrams are full of the wisdom of the farmer who warns the merchant not to sail and risk wreck. As one epitaph declares: 'From the sea I sought to gain my living, and from the sea I took out death.'

Many of the epigrams, however, deal with the pleasure of life, with eating and drinking and the love of women or boys. The repression of women in Greek society – all except prostitutes were secluded in the home – is softened in some of the epigrams by a feeling of equality in the tragedy of death, while the poems of Sappho and Erinna are admired by their fellow poets. The homosexuality of Greek men, who fixed their romantic love on boys and used their wives for breeding, needs little explanation. Since respectable women were excluded from market-place and dinner table, boys and prostitutes took their place. Demosthenes, the great Athenian orator, said publicly that every Athenian needed two mistresses as well as a wife, while homosexuality between men was given the status of virtue in myth. Did not those men who loved men merely follow the example of Achilles and Patroclus?

Above all, the epigrams show that the poverty of

Greek society had its compensation, an irony which made
life bearable. The Greeks complained of love and thought
it evil; but at least love had one virtue, it loathed a prude.
They told the story of the greedy mouse that bit at the
meat of an open oyster; its meal became its tomb. They
spoke of a man throwing a stone at a skull, put up on a
cross-roads to warn man of his fate; the stone bounced
backwards and blinded the thrower, who wept for the rest
of his life over his good aim. Such ironic detachment from
the horror of the human condition is sympathetic to our
own time which lives in daily fear of a holocaust.

The Greek Anthology is an unequalled record of a civilization. At times both savage and tender, biting and
despairing, it shows how a civilization passed from simple
faith and agriculture through defeat and degradation into
a final imperial heritage at Byzantium. The themes of the
Anthology are universal, love and life and death. The
particular subjects of the epigrams illuminate the Greek
world. As the language of classical Greece is no longer
part of a normal education, translators have the duty of
trying to explain the riches of the Greek spirit in an alien
tongue. The Anthology is a good introduction to the
classical world; it is witty, brief and exact. And if a
reading of these selected epigrams makes the reader en-
quire further into the civilization that produced them, no
translator can ask for more.

TRANSLATOR'S NOTE

I have tried my hand at a new translation and selection from the Greek Anthology for two reasons. Firstly, the change of history demands a new selection to fit our new manners; thus I have included twenty-six epigrams by the soured Palladas and only one by the idyllic Theocritus. Secondly, there exists no adequate translation of the Anthology in verse which keeps to the clarity and brevity of the original version.

The best prose translations of selected epigrams from the Greek Anthology are those of Professor J. W. Mackail and of Shane Leslie; but the prose of both men tends to be overblown and lengthy. The cutting edge of the Greek is lost. The most satisfactory verse translation is by Dudley Fitts; but although his style is admirably lucid and brief, his refusal of rhyme and his typographical tricks lose the studied metres of the Anthology.

Many of the Greek epigrams were written in an elegiac metre, a hexameter followed by a pentameter. It has been the misfortune of most verse translators of the Anthology to try to reproduce this elegiac metre in English. Edmund

Wilson, himself a poet in elegiacs, has commented on the resistance of the English language to Greek metres. Swinburne's failure to translate the Anthology stems from his over-faithful imitation of his model. Even the best-known translation from the Anthology, William Johnson Cory's version of Callimachus – *They told me, Heraclitus, they told me you were dead* – seems to me to be too galloping, jingling and verbose.

An epigram in Greek should be translated by its equivalent in English. The English epigrammatic form was developed by Elizabethan and Restoration poets. It depended for its effect on its simple metre, its form, its brevity, its clarity, and its wit. So did the Greek epigram. Therefore, I think that the elegiacs of the Anthology are best left in Greek, while an English translation should be written in a metre that suits the English epigram. Brevity demands such a choice. The incredible conciseness of the Greek makes a translator crop his own tongue to its roots. So I have chosen, on the whole, to use a line of four feet, usually trochees, and a simple rhyme-scheme of AABB or ABAB. When the epigram seems to demand a freer form, I have varied the length of my line and have replaced rhyme by assonance.

In style, I have avoided all poetic diction and old-fashioned phrases. My words are simple. I have also avoided as far as possible Greek proper names which might need an explanatory footnote (for instance, Aphrodite is habitually given the name of the Goddess of Love). I have used the usual latinized version of Greek names throughout (for instance, Meleagros is called Meleager). My intention is to make my selected epigrams easily understandable to those who have never been able to have a classical education.

My source has been W. R. Paton's exhaustive edition of *The Greek Anthology* (5 vols., London, 1916–26). I have chosen some 350 of the 4,150 epigrams. For those who wish further reading in translation, Leslie has translated 1,325 of the epigrams and Mackail 500. I have made a personal selection of those epigrams of bite and wit which seem to me to increase our understanding of ourselves and of Greek civilization. The Greeks are the fathers of our society. It is time that their children's teeth were set on edge.

ANDREW SINCLAIR

THE WRITERS
OF THE
GREEK ANTHOLOGY

AESOP

Death's the only way from living;
Man cannot flee his suffering
Nor his many sorrows bear.
Earth, sea, stars, sun and moon are fair.
But all the rest is fear and pain,
And the luck of man turns bad again.

ANACREON

Timocritus the valiant gave
His life in war. This is his grave.
War spares the coward, not the brave.

SIMONIDES

I, Brotachus from Crete, lie here.
I came not from Gortyna
To be this, but to be a trader.

No Croesus lies in the grave you see:
I was a poor labourer, and this fits me.

The God of War once washed his long-barbed arrows
In rain that was red on the breasts of these.
The standing ranks now lie beneath the barrows,
The living men are lifeless memories.

These men brought to Phoebus' coast
Spartan meats that he loved most—
One sea, one night, one ship, all lost.

On the Tomb of the Spartan Dead at Thermopylae

Stranger, tell the Spartans how we die:
Obedient to their laws, here we lie.

EMPEDOCLES

From His Book 'On Nature'

In a boy and a girl,
   The same soul can be,
In a shrub and a bird
   And a fish of the sea.

EVENUS

If hating is painful, and loving too,
The evil I choose is rose mixed with rue.

PLATO

Sailors, go safe on land and sea:
But learn, whoever you may be,
This from my tomb – The waves drowned me.

I am the tomb of a shipwrecked man.
Over the way lies a husbandman.
Death waits for us impartially
Whether on land or on the sea.

All see Time's metamorphosis. The range
Of years makes name, luck, form, and nature change.

I am Lais. My pride of face
Once laughed at all the Graecian race.
At my door, lovers stood ten deep –
Goddess of Love, my mirror keep.

As I am now, I shun my glass,
And I cannot look on who I was.

Catch the apple that I throw,
If you love me. Give me now
Your maidenhead; or if your will
Is set against me, catch it still
And think that beauty soon shall go.

MNASALCAS

Promachus gives to Phoebus now
His quiver and his crooked bow.
He gives no arrows, for they are
Already sent to the dead in war.

DIOTIMUS

'Why should I rack my belly in labour,
If I must later bury my dead?'
So his mother laid out small Bianor
When he should have buried her instead.

THEOCRITUS

Here lies the poet Hipponax.
If you are evil, keep far back.
If you are good in deed and birth,
Sit and sleep on his bed of earth.

CALLIMACHUS

*On Heraclitus of Halicarnassus, the Poet**

When they told me you were gone,
I remembered how the sun,
Heraclitus, time and again
Set on our talks: and I wept then.
Halicarnassus saw you born.
Somewhere, dust now picks your bone.
But, though Death takes everything,
Your *Nightingales* still sing, ah sing.

* Heraclitus wrote a book of poems called 'Nightingales'.

Cleombrotus the Ambracian
Said his farewell to the sun,
Leapt down to Hades from a wall,
Not because of sin at all;
But because he'd read the whole
Of Plato's treatise on the soul.

Here sleeps in holy sleep Saon
From Acanthus, Dicon's son.
The good sleep: say not they are gone.

Brief the stranger: brief my song.
In short – *Theris, Aristaeus' son,*
A Cretan. This is still too long.

Who are you, stranger, dead and drowned?
When your sandy corpse was found,
Leonticus a tombstone made
And wept for all the risks of trade.
He also travels without lull,
Restless by sea as any gull.

Trite poems are among my hates,
And roads that carry tourist trips.
I loathe a love that circulates;
Loving cups won't touch my lips.
Public things are my disgust.
'Lysanias fair, fair, fair is.'
Yet an echo stays my lust –
'Lysanias theirs, theirs, theirs is.'

THEODORIDAS

I am the tomb of a shipwrecked man:
But, stranger, sail! When we were gone,
The other ships all journeyed on.

RHIANUS

I caught the fawn, he fled away.
In vain I toiled at setting snares.
Now casual men bear off my prey —
O Passion, strike them unawares.

ASCLEPIADES

Why grudge your useless maidenhead?
For Hades holds no lovers' bed.
Love in our lives does very well,
But virgins are mere ash in Hell.

Sweet is the spring for the sailor, when winter's storm
    is over,
Sweet for the thirsty in summer is the cool drink of
    snow;
But sweeter still the time when one cloak shall cover
A pair of lovers who honour the goddess of Love also.

At play, Hermione caught and drove me.
She wore a belt of many colours
With golden letters, saying: 'Love me,
And don't you mind if I'm another's.'

Didyme waved a branch at me.
I melt as wax before her beauty.
If she is black, so's coal that glows,
When it's alight, more than the rose.

HEDYLUS

Nicagoras' wine and treachery
And dear love lulled Aglaonicē.
Here she has left for Love's goddess
Her sandals and her maiden dress,
So they may true witness keep
Of his violence and her sleep.

POSEIDIPPUS (or ASCLEPIADES)

Cleander on Cytherea's beach
Saw Nico swimming out of reach.
He burned with love, took to his breast
Dry coals from her wet nakedness.
He was wrecked upon the sand,
While she was washed up on the land.

Equal their love now. Granted be
The prayers of those who watch the sea.

POSEIDIPPUS
(or Plato the Comic Poet)

Which way of life should suit a man?
The market sweats him all it can.
Home gives anxieties to bear:
The land means work, the sea means fear.
To travel rich risks loss of all:
To travel poor is unbearable.
The married man has too much care:
But lonely is the bachelor.
Children make your life a mess,
Yet crippled he who is childless.
Young men are fools, old men are weak,
Which leaves two choices so to speak: —
Either don't be born at all
Or breathe your last at your first bawl.

METRODORUS

An answer to Poseidippus
(or Plato the Comic Poet)

All ways of life should suit a man.
The market aids him all it can.
At home, there's rest and perfect health:
The land means beauty, sea means wealth.
To travel rich means fame and fun:
To travel poor is to go anon.
The married man has the best of houses:
But the bachelor does what he chooses.
Children bring you happiness,
Yet carefree he who is childless.
Young men are strong, old men can pray,
Which leaves no choices so to say
Between not being born and dying.
Living is well worth the trying.

LEONIDAS OF TARENTUM

Man, you passed through infinity
Before your birth, and you will see
The same eternity when you die.
The rest of your life is the prick of a pin
Or less, if there be a smaller thing.
Little your living, and all suffering.
Even your few days cannot be happy.
They are far worse than Death the Enemy.
You are skin and bone, yet you fly high.
But what's the use? For the worm sucks in
The meat of the leaf to help him spin.
Less than a web, the leaf hangs thin.
Man, count your strength at each new day.
Be content to go a simple way,
And remember, while you stay
Alive, your self is straw and clay.

Old Maronis, who dried pots,
Loved what was in them. On her tomb,
An Attic cup reveals her plots.
The poor children of her womb
And her husband pass her by:
She weeps because the cup is dry.

These great Lucanian shields, this row
Of bridles, this forked shine of spear
Are hung to Pallas. Black death now
Eats horse and man. They are not here.

A wallet, the hard skin of a goat,
A walking-stick, a filthy flask
For oil, a doggy purse (and in it
Not a penny), and a hat
For a godless head – Famine hung the lot
On the bushes of a tamarisk.
There lies Sochares. That is that.

Goddess of Love, accept these things
From Leonidas, the wanderer,
The penniless. His offerings
Are barley-cakes, olives from the store,
A green fig, five from a bunch of grapes.
The dregs of wine are his sacrifice.
You have kept him well. If he escapes
Poverty, a kid shall be your prize.

A little dust upon my head
Is enough for me.
Sarcophagi oppress the dead.
Let such for others be.
Calliteles gat Alexander –
But now that I am gone
What's the use for them that wander
To read this on my tomb?

I lie far from Italy,
Far from Tarentum, my country.
Death could not be bitterer:
This is the ill of the wanderer.
But the Muses loved my rhyme:
Instead of sourness sweets are mine.
The name Leonidas is not lost,
But to posterity has passed.

THYMOCLES

Remember, remember, my holy words –
'Fairest beauty is most fleet.'
Beauty outstrips the swiftest birds.
Your blossoms lie about your feet.

DIONYSIUS THE SOPHIST

Rose-girl, there are roses
    Also in you.
What do you sell? Your roses?
    Yourself? The two?

CRATES

Love's death is caused by hunger:
If not, time does the murder.
But if the fire yields to neither,
A rope's end is your answer.

ANTIPATER OF SIDON

Toiling ant, I build a mound
Of earth for you by the threshing-floor,
So that in death you may adore
The furrow which the harvest bore,
And the plough that tilled the ground.

According to astrologers,
I Seleucus have few years
To live. But I don't care, for if
My way to Hell is rather brief,
It's the same way for us all.
I'll just pay Death an earlier call.
Water-drinkers walk the course,
But wine-bibbers take a horse.

Bitto gave back to Athene
The singing comb that wove her loom
And her bare life. 'Your gift, Athene,
I give up, though I am come
To forty. Love is now my rage;
Lust is stronger still than age.'

ARCHIAS (or PARMENION)

I am Echo, who can hold her tongue.
So watch your words, as you go and come.
If you say That, then I'll say That:
Tit for Tit, and Tat for Tat.
If you'll be silent, then I must.
Who could have a tongue more just?

ARCHIAS OF MYTILENE

Praise be the Thracians, for they mourn
Each Thracian child when he is born.
But when Fate sends her servant Death,
They bless each man on his last breath.
The living suffer evilly.
The dead have found the remedy.

MELEAGER

Morning Star, who brings the dawn,
   Quickly come again,
Changed into the Evening Star,
   Bringing her who's gone.

While still a baby in his mother's lap,
Love lost my soul this morning, shooting craps.

Holy Lamp and Night, we both
Swore by you to keep our oath.
He swore to love, I not to leave;
You witnessed there was no reprieve.
These words of his were writ on rivers.
The Lamp sees him fall on other lovers.

Love's din ever plagues my ears.
Desire pricks my silent tears.
Night and day, the insomnia
Of passion brands my heart with fire.
Winged Love, is it that you may
Fly to us, but not away?

Asclepias loves love. The summer sea
That blues her eye tempts all to try love's journey.

Mosquito, be my messenger,
Fly to whine in Zenophila's ear:
'He waits for you, sweet slug-a-bed,
While you forget with sleepyhead.'
Tssng! Go, dear piper, go! Speak low!
Don't wake her jealous bed-fellow!
Bring her back, mosquito, please,
And with skin and club you'll be Hercules.

The lip of the wine-cup is sweet.
It tells of the touch of the mouth
Of Zenophila, prattling of love.
Happy cup! If she could set
Her lips to my lips, she would quaff
My soul in one swallow of love.

As the flowers fade on Heliodora's hair,
The flowers in her skin grow still more fair.

Love sharpened Heliodora's nail;
For her light scratches score my soul.

Love moulded Heliodora in my skin;
Soul of my soul, her sweet words speak within.

Love, I pray you, call a truce.
If I Heliodora choose
And cannot sleep, yet rest your bow,
Find other targets for your arrow.
Or I'll dying say: 'O stranger,
Look at love the murderer.'

MELEAGER (possibly PHILODEMUS)

My soul says – Flee from Heliodora,
Her love brings tears and jealousy.
I disobey, because the more the
Shameless girl bids me ignore her,
All the more she kisses me.

MELEAGER

I mocked the songs of wailing lovers,
    Then Myiscus caught me.
Winged Love has branded me all over –
    'Plunder Won From Chastity.'

I, seeing Thero, am all-seeing,
Yet if I but see everything,
Not Thero, then I see nothing.

Timarion, your eyes are fire,
    Bird-lime your lips.
Your look burns me with desire,
    Your touch entraps.

Earth, who mothers all, Aesigenes
Put no burden on you. For his ease,
Burden his body lightly where it lies.

Clearista on her marriage bed
Took off the girdle of a maid;
But death came in her husband's stead.
Flutes at her door were sweetly played;
Yet soon the sound was rapping hands.
The bridal song became a knell.
She took the self-same burning brands
That ringed her bed as lights to Hell.

At eighteen, you, Charixenus, wore
A shroud to warm you under earth.
The stones moaned loud, while your friends bore
Your corpse away. You married Death.
Those breasts are dry that gave you suck:
That bloody birth of yours was vain.
The evil, barren maiden, Luck,
Spat out your mother's love and pain.
All that is left for friends to do
Is to mourn, while your parents wail,
While those who were unknown to you
Add their pity to the tale.

ZONAS

From this sweet cup of clay, let me be fed.
From clay I came, in clay I shall lie dead.

ERYCIUS OF CYZICUS

Demetrius fled the fight in fear.
And lost his weapons. Once at home,
His mother stabbed him with a spear
Through his side, and said to him:

'Die. Let Sparta feel no shame.
My milk fed cowards in her name.'

CRINAGORAS

A mason built this monument
Of polished marble, true and fair;
But no good man is resident.
Don't judge the dead by what they wear.
Stone has no sense, for it can hide
Black dung as well as anything.
Weak Eunicides lies inside:
Beneath the ash is a rotten thing.

On a Skull

Roof without tongue, pan without brain,
Crown without hair, shell without eye,
Bone without grave, the passers-by
Weep to see you where you lie
Near the tree-trunk, for we spy
That scrimping life has little gain.

Merciless Death, you take from Evander
His daughter Hymnis, the whole house's friend,
A nine years' old pet. Why do you demand her
So early, if she is yours in the end?

The washerwoman on the beach
Above the rocks was swept away
By a flooding wave, which drowned the wretch.
She drank the salt of death that day.
One gulp put her beyond the reach
Of living and of poverty.

On a ship, who dares to stand,
When the sea can kill upon the land?

ANTIPATER OF THESSALONICA

Tears can't quench love, Telembrotus:
No water can such a fire douse.
Gold is the cure of Love. For He
Was born quite dry upon the sea.

This is the place where Leander crossed over.
These are the straits that drowned other lovers.
These are the ruins of Hero's tower.
Here the lamp stood, treacherous to her.
In this same tomb, the two lie together,
Still blaming the envy of wind and weather.

The slave-child of Hippocrates
Crawled from his cottage to the sea.
And died from sucking this new breast.
The sea's a worse mother than the rest.

'Children are a woman's prayer,'
Polyxo cried. Then she gave birth
To three boys. Through her belly's tear,
A midwife slid them onto earth.
The children lived; dead was their mother.
God gave them life and killed another.

I am a plane-tree, dry and dead.
A vine climbs over me, who once
As many leaves and clusters fed.
But now I wear her radiance.

So rare a mistress men should find
To grace their death, unlike her kind.

I fear the storm that's gathering,
Waves pounding rock and lightning,
Less than the water-drinker's ears
Which record the words he hears.

ANTIPATER (OF THESSALONICA?)

Cythere from Bithynia
Gave this marble goddess here
To Love divine. Give back to her
Much for little: keep her dear
To her husband, close, together.

Those who loved death in battle won no grave
Like other men; but brave men hymn the brave.

ANTIPATER (OF THESSALONICA?)
(or Plato)

By the roadside, they planted me,
The butt of boys, a walnut tree.
Their stones break off each twig and leaf.
The rain is flint that feeds my life.
What good is fruit to us on earth?
I only bore the fruit of death.

HONESTUS

I do not wish to marry hag or child.
The young I pity, and revere the old.
A sour grape or raisin won't be mine,
Only a beauty ripening on the vine.

On a Tombstone

I bear the name of Timocles
And wonder, as I scan the sea,
Where his corpse is. Long since, the fish
Have eaten him, while I languish,
A useless stone, carved uselessly.

APOLLONIDES

Blind Timoclea, blind no longer
Now you have twin boys, not one.
Through their four eyes, your sight is stronger –
You look, perfected, on the Sun.

Who has not endured the worst,
Lamenting one among his sons?
In four days, Poseidippus lost
His hopes and all four boys at once.

The father wept away his sight:
Now all are held in a common night.

Gold hung on the neck of the Captain,
Valiant Aelius the Roman.
He remembered his past glory,
When he lay wasted with paralysis.
He fell upon his sword, and said: 'We die,
Cowards by sickness, but men like this.'

MARCUS ARGENTARIUS

Psyllus brought a whorish stable
To entertain young men in style.
He preyed on weakness, and was able
To deal in flesh and make his pile.
He lies dead here. But don't throw stones,
Traveller, nor urge on others.
Spare the complacent pander's bones –
He kept young men from seducing mothers.

Her breast against my breast, her skin on mine,
Her lip against my lip, with nothing in
Between Antigone and me, we lay.
I say no more. The rest the lamp can say.

I loved a girl called Alcippē,
And talked her round, and secretly
Brought her to bed. We hid and feared
Our loving might be overheard.
Her mother soon popped in her head,
'My daughter, we go halves,' she said.

'Dioclea has little breasts,
But sweet her other interests.'
'Not much can keep us, then, apart:
I'll lie the closer to her heart.'

Melissa, I do quite agree
You should be named after the bee.
Your kiss is a sweet and honied thing,
But your price reveals your sting.

ALPHEIUS OF MYTILENE

Unhappy they who cannot love;
They find it hard to speak or move.
Yet if I saw Xenophilus,
Lightning would lag behind my swiftness.
Let sweet desire be your goal –
Love is the whetstone of the soul.

AMMIANUS

At another's table, don't appear,
Filling your belly with shameful bread,
Matching laugh for laugh and tear for tear,
When you feel neither glad nor sad.

Your beard grows brains, your theory is:
So you let it grow to flap at flies.
Shave it off, take my advice:
The things that grow in beards are lice.

Earth, lie light on that wretch Nearchus,
So dogs can easily chew his carcass.

LUCILIUS

Asclepiades the miser
    Said to a mouse:
'My dear, what are you doing
    Here in my house?'
The mouse said merrily:
    'Friend, fear no fraud.
I am here to look for
    A bed, not board.'

Once Antiochus laid his eyes
   On Lysimachus' cushion,
Lysimachus never laid his eyes
   On his cushion again.

Through Diophantes' ship, the tide
And oceans flow without a care.
Between the decks, the dolphins ride
And mermaids comb their shining hair.
Soon someone will set sail inside
Our hull, as all the sea's in there.

   Eutychus the painter
   Has got twenty sons,
   But as for a likeness,
   He never got it once.

Astrologer on astrologer
Said my uncle would live forever.
Hermoclides said that he'd die soon
The moment he was already gone.

Giaus was so very light,
He would not have arrived,
Had he not attached a weight
To his foot before he dived.

Miser Hermon played the rake
In his sleep, but, once awake,
Hanged himself for his mistake.

Lazy Marcus ran a race
In his sleep and stayed sleepless
For fear of having to run twice.

Fellow boxers set on high
Apis' statue here. And why?
Because he never hurt a fly.

Augustus, once Olympicus,
Had ears, chin, forehead, eyelids, nose.
But, taking up a boxer's stance,
He lost with them his inheritance.
He was taken for another,
Less like himself than was his brother.

You bought hair, rouge, cream, teeth and paste.
It'd cost the same to buy a face.

Nicylla's hair is coal-black hair.
It's dyed, says the voice of slander.
In fact, she bought it over the counter.

LUCILIUS
(or Menecrates of Samos)

If an old man prays to go on living,
He deserves decades of slowly dying.

LUCILIUS (or POLEMO OF PONTUS)

Eros, put an end to loving,
Or see that we are loved;
Either make desire a nothing,
Or mutually proved.

NICARCHUS

When the raven sings at night,
    Death passes by.
But when they hear Demophilus,
    The ravens die.

Does Diodorus fart or yawn?
The smell of both is just the same.

Doctor Marcus laid his hand
  On a stone God yesterday.
Though He's both stone and divine,
  They bury Him today.

Niconoë was once a beauty,
But well before the Flood.
She's so old our memory
Can't see her as we should.

But now she ought to set her course,
Not for a husband, but a hearse.

ANTIPHILUS OF BYZANTIUM

A file's iron teeth turned gold to dust,
Lighter than the sands of Libya.
A small mouse ate the golden crust.
This made his belly heavier,
And slowed his paws. So he was caught
And cut in two and lost his loot
And life. Gold has ever brought
Evil alike to man and brute.

When I was dead, they gave me burial;
Now my bones bleach where wheat shall yellow.
Once I was laid out with due funeral;
Now the iron share ploughs me below.

Stranger, who said that death ended pain,
When even the tomb yields me again?

I said near harbour: 'The foul wind
Will be tomorrow's breeze behind.'
No more had I time to tell
Because the sea fell down to Hell.
One small sound caused me endless sorrow –
Never speak the word 'tomorrow'.
For such little things as this
Are always heard by Nemesis.

Adventure thought up ships to tread
The roads of the sea – their dust is wealth.
Yet wooden ships drown men by stealth,
And death is the only friend of greed.

Golden the lives of mortals are,
If the sea, like Hell, is seen from far.

AUTOMEDON OF CYZICUS

In the evening, men take wine together.
In the morning, beasts prey on each other.

BASSUS

I refuse to become a shower of gold,
A bull or a swan as in days of old.
Let Zeus do tricks. Corinna's more willing,
If I remain human and give her a shilling.

BIANOR

Look at this man, a worm, a slave,
   A nothing.
Yet he has another's soul
   As his thing.

DIODORUS

Diogenes, when the North wind broke
His yard-arm off Carpathia
In darkness, vowed this little cloak

To you, Cabirus of Boeotia,
If he lived. He did. One thing more.
You let him live. Let him not be poor.

LEONIDAS OF ALEXANDRIA

I am a ship that sailed the distant sea.
I came to Mother Earth. She showed no mercy.
She burned her pines that were my ribs. I found
Deep sea more faithful than the faithless ground.

EVODUS

On a Statue of Echo

Echo is a mimic, the dregs of the voice:
She puts a tail on the head of every noise.

ISIDORUS OF AEGAE

I am Eteocles, whom the sea
Drew from my farm to make of me
A merchant. I was setting sail
When a fierce Tyrrhenian gale
Sunk my ship in a sudden squall.
My new trade was unnatural.
The wind that blows the chaff from wheat
Is not the same that blows a boat.

JULIUS POLYAENUS

Hope blinds us to the going
Of minutes one by one.
The day of our undoing,
We leave too much undone.

PARMENION

A child was peering from the edge
Of a tiled roof – Death does not have
Terrors for youth. Behind the ledge,
Its mother bared her breast which gave,
Life twice to one who lipped the grave.

To marry a hag or starve
Is a difficult choice to have.
Hunger is a thing to dread,
But worse an old maid in your bed.
Phillis, starving out his life,
Prayed to find an aged wife.
But on the day he slept with her,
He prayed again for his hunger.
Fickle is the man who's born
Without his fair share of income.

I need my cloak to cover me:
My food is the fare of poetry.
I do not ask for much to eat.
For wealth gives flattery its meat,
And no one else. Damn patronage!
Free is the man who needs no wage.

PHILIPPUS

Old Nico laid, upon the earth
Over young Melitē, a wreath.
Where is the righteousness of Death?

From huntsman Gelo, Pan now gets
A spear made blunt by blood and time,
Old rags in twisted hunting-nets,
Nooses that choke the necks of game,
Sinews that nip the legs of beasts,
Collars round dogs that point their nose.
His greatest strength becomes his least.
His hunting-hill is now repose.

LUCIAN

If you're slow to run and quick to eat,
Run with your mouth and eat with your feet.

To mortals is mortality.
All things must pass us by.
If not, we pass them by.

It's not Love that does men evil.
They blame on Love their inner devil.

Squander as if you'd die tomorrow.
Scrape as if you had nine lives.
Wise the man who tries to follow
Both of these imperatives
And neither much nor little gives.

All life is short for the fortunate;
But when men are unfortunate
One night-time is infinite.

Acindynus swore he'd stay sober,
While all the rest drank up their sense.
Thus he found he was thought the only
Man who was under the influence.

Harsh Death took me, Callimachus.
I was not five, and I was heedless.
Yet do not cry for me. For if I knew
Little of life, my woes were little too.

PTOLEMY

I know I am human, a thing of one day:
But when in the heavens I see each star
Spiral in his galaxy, then away!
My feet stand with Zeus, my lips drink nectar.

RUFINUS

Love cannot wise hearts undo.
I can counter his attack.
Men can throw immortals too.
But if Wine battles at his back,
How can I resist the two?

Love's act performed, no charm survives,
Else men would ever take their wives,
If they were able to adore
As much after as before.

If Europa's lips but touch your lips
Or brush your mouth, sweet is her kiss;
But she will closer cling than this
And suck your soul from your finger-tips.

Alone I chanced on Prodikē,
Cupped the ambrosia of her knee,
Said: 'Save a man who's nearly lost!
Pity the last breath of a ghost!'
She wept, but wiped away the tear
And gently pushed me off from her.

Prodikē, I warned you, age is coming,
Love is lagging and dissolving.
Wrinkles like harpies hold you in,
Crab mouth, grey hair, tired flesh, dry skin.

Who wants you now, my haughty one –
We pass you like a roadside tomb.

I send this wreath, my Rhodoclea,
Made by my hands from every flower.
Lily and rose and anemone,
Narcissus and violet woven lie.
Wear it, and put off your pride.
The wreath and you both bloom and fade.

Thalia, I have often prayed
That, as now, you might be laid
With your sweet body in my bed,
So my passion could be fed.
But a tiredness clogs my flesh!
Wake, my spirit, new and fresh!
Some day you will seek in vain
To find this ecstasy again.

STRATO

Who can tell if his loved lover
   Pass his prime,
If the lovers pass together
   All their time?
Yesterday shall bring today
   The same delight.
Tomorrow too, if we but stay
   Within sight.

If your beauty must be gone,
Give it me soon, give it me soon.
But O, if your beauty stays,
Give me what you'll have always.

If you think my kiss is a sin and a shame,
Punish my sin by returning the same.

I like all young men. I will not choose
   A brother from a brother
For his beauty. One for one charm I use,
   Another for another.

A white-skinned boy is the death of me.
A brown-skinned boy burns me with honey.
But a fair-haired boy melts me utterly.

Cyris, why rest your body on the wall?
Why tempt the stone, when it's incapable?

Heliodorus, kissing's a pleasure
If it's lip for lip, and measure for measure,
But if your lips stay closed and slack,
I'd rather a dummy kissed me back.

Last evening, when we said adieu,
   Moeris kissed me.
Did I dream or was it true?
   Nothing missed me.
What he said or asked I knew;
   But if he kissed me,
How can I, turned to a God,
Walk the earth where he has trod?

As you read these trifles over,
You'll think these pangs of love were mine.
In fact, I scribble for any old lover,
Since God gave me the gift of rhyme.

ST GREGORY THE THEOLOGIAN

Orators, speak now. This tomb has sealed the lips
Of the great orator Amphilocus.

Noble Caesarius, you who gave
All to your brothers from your small grave,
You knew the Stars and Geometry
And Medicine, and yet you die.

On Tomb-Robbers

Break in, break in, all you that have a lust
For stones. The treasure of this tomb is dust.

GLYCON

All is dust and all is laughter,
    All is trivial.
Chaos before and chaos after,
    Unreason hatches all.

PALLADAS

Unlucky Greeks, are we not dead,
Seeming alive, by dreaming fed?
Or do we live and is life dead?

You say you're rich. So what?
Will your hearse hold all you've got?
What you're getting that you're giving,
Making money loses living.

I'm not hurt by poverty,
Yet it damns me in your eye.
It's my luck that's bad, not I.

Praise makes a friend, blame makes an enemy,
Yet to speak ill of others is Attic honey.

Why babble, you who'll soon be dead?
Shut your mouth! Rehearse instead
The peace that cannot be gainsaid.

Why reduce the Universe
    To a decimal,
When your body's little earth
    Is infinitesimal?
Why not set your calculus
    On Self first of all?
Count yourself and know yourself
    Before the uncountable.
A man's measure is his matter,
    Then the immeasurable.

He who hates the man God loves
Does all the follies that he can.
For he fights his God above
With his envy in his hand.
Better far to love the man.

From king to beggar,
We fatten on our feet.
Hogs for the butcher,
We die like any meat.

In tears I came,
With tears I go,
Finding the whole
World tearful too.
Weak men, sad men,
So full of tears,
You are washed away
Though hardly here.

Live your sad life without a word,
For time is wordless too.
Also live unseen, unheard,
For when you die, you do.

If Luck blows a gale,
Then ride the tide.
For if you rebel,
You must still ride.

The poor man has no death,
For life no living gave.
While he appeared to breathe
The wretch was in his grave.
Dying can only touch
The rich in all they have.

The thought of dying makes you sweat.
But when you're dead you're free of it.
So please don't weep as men must go –
They do not suffer down below.

I was born bare
And bare I'll go.
Why work at all
When you know
That you'll end so?

Goddam the belly and its food.
Because of them, the good are lewd.

Flattery's father, you are gold.
You are the son of pain and care.
Fearful the man you enfold,
Suffering the man you leave bare.

Every woman is annoying,
Yet twice she's ripe and red:
The first time when she's marrying,
The second when she's dead.

The man cursed with an ugly wife sees night
Each evening when the candles are alight.

God gave fire twice to man:
First was flame and second woman.
Damn both! Though we can douse a blaze,
Woman flares and burns always.

If monks are solitary, why so many?
If monks are many, why so solitary?
Of one conversion monks are proud,
Solitude's become a crowd.

Every morning we are born,
Nothing of our life is left.
For yesterday is gone away.
Daily we begin afresh.
No man is too old to be told:
Forget past years and live the rest.

This is life and nothing else is.
Life is pleasure. Damn dull care!
Man shall live no more than this.
Now, there's wine and women fair,
Flowers and dance. Live well today:
What comes tomorrow none can say.

A man went to bed with a grammarian's daughter.
Her child was masculine, feminine and neuter.

You say you're a know-all
But you're good at blow all.
The dabbler eternal
Is never original.

Pythagoras the eloquent
Knew the wisdom of the silent.
The secret of all rhetoric –
His pupils learned – was not to speak.

Remember, man, your father's cock.
Does vanity survive the shock?
Or does Platonic flattery
Persuade you heaven's in the sky?
'Of dust thou art, to dust return. . .'

But that's a pompous way to learn.
I'll put it straight. You're born of luck,
A lick of lust and a mite of muck.

DAMASCIUS THE PHILOSOPHER

A slave was Zosimē
In her body only,
And now her body's free.

ERATOSTHENES SCHOLASTICUS

Fair is a virgin's treasury;
But if all are virgin, where are we?
So marry, and replace your body
With others, but shun lechery.

Bacchus, this empty cask receive.
It is all drunk Xenophon has to leave.

AGATHIAS SCHOLASTICUS

Why do you fear Death,
The mother of sleep?
She cures the sick,
Quiets them that weep.
She visits once only,
She does not come twice.
But disease comes often
In many a guise.

Your body's like a shadow,
No thicker than the wind,
So never touch your neighbour
Lest he prove unkind
And breathe you up his nostrils
Not noticing you're there.
You needn't fear your dying –
Already you're thin air.

Pan loves the woods and rocks: he got
From Charicles a yellow goat –
Horn for horn, and hairs for hairs,
Leap for leap, both foresters.

Without the marriage bed, no need
Would exist to make us breed.
In the poor woman's labouring womb
A child lay dead in its sad room.
Three days passed by: the child stayed there,
Hoping in vain to breathe the air.
The womb serves him in place of earth;
Flesh is the dust that hides his birth.

On a Former Magistrate

Where is your illimitable pride?
Where the massed flatterers at your side?
Now that you're exiled far from your city,
Luck makes those judge who were judged by your pity.
Then good luck to Luck, who mocks at us all,
Causing our rise but to laugh at our fall.

On a Dice Game

This is a game, yet in the dice
Fortune is shown and her caprice.
Now you win and now you lose.
This is life's fickleness you choose.
Praise to the man who lives and plays,
Moderate in joy and grief always.

On a Mosquito Net

The job of nets is to ensnare
Quick-winged small creatures; but my care
Is to chase them off, not close them round,
To keep them distant. safe and sound.
No mosquito, buzzing small,
Can pierce me for his funeral.
The winged I save, and men can trust
Their sleep to me. Who is more just?

On a House in Byzantium

Musonius worked both long and late
On this great house, lashed by the wind.
Now he knows the black house of Fate
And lives below, leaves me behind.
In earth's narrow bed he lies,
While I am the joy of strangers' eyes.

On a Lavatory in the Suburbs of Smyrna

All that rich food and living meant
Becomes here stinking excrement.
Pheasants and fish to tempt the tongue,
Pastry and *gateaux*, now are dung.
The gullet gulps, the belly rids
Itself of all its costly solids.
At last man's foolish pride is hurt: –
He's spent his gold to make more dirt.

Pillars, portraits and monuments
Delight the living who possess them;
But fame and glory have no sense
For the dead who do not miss them.
Virtue and wisdom go with us
Or stay behind as memory.
Plato and Homer reason thus
And leave no likeness when they die.

Blessed is he, who in wise books
Survives, and not in empty looks.

JULIANUS, PREFECT OF EGYPT

Rhodo, your sweet husband makes
A marble tomb to house your body.
He gives alms for your kind soul's sake;
For you died young and set him free.

You died not from the tempest's furies;
You were made mad by griping greed.
Let others profit from stormy seas;
The land can give me what I need.

The painter caught Theodetē
In the full flush of her beauty.
If his brush had failed, then we
Who weep might lose our memory.

While wreathing roses, Love I found
  Upon a flowery bank.
I caught him by the wings and drowned
  Him in wine, and drank.
Now, within my belly bound,
  He tickles me in thanks.

Nymphs, take the net of Cinyras.
His casting arm has lost its prowess.
Now the fish feed happily,
For his old age has freed the sea.

On an Unguarded House

Robbers, look for wealthier houses.
Poverty's the watchdog over this.

MACEDONIUS THE CONSUL

Praise to remembering,
Forgetting also.
Memory for the good thing.
Oblivion for woe.

Constant your name, inconstant your doing.
When I heard you called Constant, I thought you
    might be.
But death is no crueller. You fly from all wooing
After him who despises you, only to flee
Once he also loves you. I bit on the tip
Of the barb in your mouth. Now I hang from your lip.

The laughing girl came in my dream.
She gave herself to my caprice;
But jealous love chose a device
To combat me by stratagem.
A nightmare spilt my cup of bliss,
And woke me. Love's envy can
Never concede to any man,
Even in dreams, his happiness.

Bees do not plough nor dig their honey;
They bribe the flowers of the spring.
So I work at Love with money,
Which culls the sweetest offering.

I gave up hope. You came. This thing
Has drained my soul's imagining.
Passion makes my deep heart quiver.
Love has drowned this mariner.
But save me, now I near the shore,
And be my harbour evermore.

You say you'll see me on the morrow.
It never comes; and so you borrow
More time to put off my desire.
Lover to some, to me a liar,
You say we'll meet this evening;
But the eve of woman's a wrinkled thing.

On an Inn in Cibyra

I love stranger and native equally.
It's not the job of hospitality
To ask who, and what, and from where you may be.

PAULUS SILENTIARIUS

I squeeze her breasts, our mouths are one,
I lick her neck like a silver spoon.
And yet I cannot call the tune;
All except her bed is won.

Love yields her breasts, sense locks her thighs,
And in between, my passion dies.

When a mad dog bites a man,
He sees its snarl in every pool.
Has Love got rabies, that it can
With its bite make me a fool?

For I see the love that's mine
In sea and stream and cup of wine.

Sweet, my friends, is Lais' smile,
Sweet the tears that milk her eye.
Yesterday, she put awhile
Her head on me and gave a sigh.

I asked, 'Why do you weep?' She said,
'Men lie and leave. I am afraid.'

Philinna, I would rather choose
Your wrinkles than more youthful juice.
Your clustered apples in my palms
Are more to me than firm, young arms.
Autumn can joy and spring can kill,
Winter can burn and summer chill.

Rhodope, let's steal our kisses
And much more. For love's true bliss is
To be unseen by all and any:
Furtive lovers taste the honey.

'My name is . . .' '*Do we care?*'
'I came from . . .' '*Anywhere.*'
'Noble my blood and race.'
'*And if it were a disgrace?*'
'A righteous life I had.'
'*What if your life was bad?*'
'Here does my body lie.'
'*Who are you, voice? Or I?*'

CONSTANTINUS CEPHALAS

As I must teach the joy of learning
To the young, I'll start with Love:
For his torch is always burning,
Sparking the thoughts that young men move.

WRITERS
OF
UNKNOWN DATE

ADDAEUS

If you see a beauty,
Strike while you can.
Don't start on a parley,
Lust is made for man.
Once you are friendly,
Hiding your wooing,
Shame is your enemy,
Stopping your doing.

CALLICTER

Phidon did not feel me over
Nor purge my bowels inside.
The very day I caught a fever,
I remembered him and died.

A girl earns her nest-egg not by trade,
But by the natural way she's made.

CAPITO

Beauty catches but a look,
Not a heart, if there's no charm.
It's like bait without a hook;
It floats and does no harm.

DIOPHANES OF MYRINA

Love is three times a thief in his lair.
He is sleepless and reckless and strips us bare.

DIOSCORIDES

Dēmaeneta sent eight sons
To fight the ranks of the foe.
She buried them all at once,
Her mourning saw no tears flow.

One sentence she said only:
'Sparta, I bore them for thee.'

HELLADIUS

Dyer, who dyes the whole world's hue,
You've dyed your rags to riches too.

ISODORUS SCHOLASTICUS
OF BOLBYTINE?

Moon, your friend Endymion
Gives the vain bed he lies on
To you. His hair is gone all grey,
And his past beauty fled away.

JOANNES THE POET

Nosto, your virtue gained this thing alone:
Your husband wept tears to find you gone.

MENECRATES

When youth has cares,
It prays for age,
But men of years
Loathe the stage
Of growing grey.
Age only lures
When far away.

NICODEMUS (OR BASSUS)

All mankind praised Hippocrates.
He saved the people of great cities.
Death was short of men in Hades.

NICOMACHUS

This is – This was Plateaea.
An earthquake destroyed her.
Little was left, and we, the dead,
Take our town as stones on our head.

PLATO THE YOUNGER

The blind man humps the lame man like a pack.
He lends his feet, his eyes he borrows back.

STATYLLIUS FLACCUS (OR PLATO)

A man left his halter,
On finding gold.
He found the halter
Who of old
Had left the gold,
And did not falter.
He hanged himself
For loss of wealth
Upon the halter.

STATYLLIUS FLACCUS

Flaccus gave me, this lamp of silver,
To faithless Napē, as a friend
Of their love; but now I quiver
To watch her lewdness without end.
As I droop beside her bed,
Wretched Flaccus twists and turns;
For although we find we're parted,
The same care burns us, cruelly burns.

ZELOTUS (OR BASSUS)

I am a pine. On land, the wind wrecked me.
Why choose me for a second wreck by sea?

ANONYMOUS
EPIGRAMS

ON LOVE

I kissed her and she favoured me:
I had her and our passion grows.
But who am I and who is she?
And why at all? Love only knows.

O, to be wind on the shore
Where you strip your breasts bare
And feel me as I blow there.

I send you scent, which is not fit
To honour you. You honour it,
Because you make the scent smell sweet.

Woman is more than man in loving.
But out of shame she hides love's sting.
Although she's mad for that very thing.

Sthenelais sets the town on fire,
Makes us breathe gold for our desire.
Her price is high. But all the night,
I dreamed she lay for my delight,
Naked in bed and all for free.
Now she'll see no more of me.
No more I'll rage at her, for Sleep
Can give me what she likes to keep.

You who love boys, give up your lust.
Perverted ones, give up your pain.
Frustration drives us mad. The dust
Of Libya counted grain by grain,
The ocean drained, these tasks are small,
When love of boys can still command
Men's souls, and gods'. Look at me, all –
My sweat is water on the sand.

Sylvanus has two servants,
Wine and Sleep adoring.
His friends and the Muses
He now finds boring.
Wine drives him from his bed,
Sleep keeps him there snoring.

Conan is only three feet tall,
His wife is double that,
When their feet are on a level
In bed, what does he look at?

(Some attribute the epigram above to Julian the Apostate.)

You must know that a rich old woman,
Placianus, is a gilded coffin.

I know enough
To love them that love me,
To hate them that hate me –
I have tried both.

ON LIVING

Enjoy your prime;
All things decline.
A summertime
Turns kid to goat.

Apollophanes, you're poor,
Let him call you rich who dares.
Spending riches means they're yours,
Saving them means they're your heir's.

How born? Where from? Why here? To go?
How can I learn, who nothing know?
From nothing come, I'll nothing find;
Good for nothing is mankind.
So serve the cup that Bacchus fills –
This is the antidote for ills.

Borrow and yourself amuse –
Let the money-lender's fingers
Swell with cramps as he lingers
Counting up your I.O.U.'s.

For those who leave the light, I do not cry;
I cry for those who daily wait to die.

A useful servant's good to use,
But serving self has less to lose.

It's sweet to thank at once. To thank too late
Turns gratitude to an ingrate.

Heliodorus, he is clever
Who keeps good friends as friends for ever.

A married man who tries another wife,
Like a wrecked sailor, risks again his life.

Untimely is excess in all.
A proverb damns the prodigal –
Too much honey turns to gall.

Doctor Crateas and Damon the sexton
Plotted for their advantage.
Damon stole the shrouds for Crateas
To use instead of a bandage.
While Crateas requested Damon
To bury off his carnage.

Alcimenes, in his small garden,
Ate his fill all summer there.
So he brought to Pan a burden
Of water, apple, fig and prayer:
'You allow me from your bounty

The good of life. So please accept
These fruits and water. Then grant me
Even more than you have kept.'

I was poor and young. Now I'm rich and old.
Alone of men, grief has been my gold.
When I needed money, I hadn't a penny:
Now I have money, I can't use any.

Sweet wine at the bottom of a jar
Turns to bitter vinegar.
Once old men empty life's last hour
Their tempers also curdle sour.

Youth and age are both loathsome.
One is gone and one must come.

Hell holds Tantalus and judgement.
This I believe, because my want
Trains me for the Inferno's torment.

Do not call the living heirs,
Now the dead have all that's theirs.
They have a great inheritance:
The end of this life of mischance.

Grey time creeps by. He is dumb.
He steals the voice of speaking men.
Unseen, he makes the seen unseen,
And causes the unseen to come.

O life, your end is out of mind,
As, day by day, men crawl on blind!

ON DEATH

You can start from Athens,
Meroe or anywhere.
It's a straight road to Hades,
Once you're dead, you'll get there.
The same wind blows to Hades
For native and stranger.

Leaves paint the trees,
Stars point the sky.
Earth praises Greece,
These men their country.

Time wears stone and blisters iron,
His sickle cuts all things that are.
By cold rain, the grave is worn
That holds Laertes near the shore.

But heroes live eternally,
For time is dimmed by poetry.

I am dead, but wait for you.
You shall wait for another too.
Death undoes all men can do.

On a Woman

Here I lie, famous, beneath this stone,
Because I gave myself to one man alone.

What if the fates in heaven fix
That I should die at thirty-six?
I am content. It is the pride
Of life, and even Nestor died.

Farewell, Hope and Lady Luck,
You'll see no more of me.
I'm home at last, my anchor's struck.
And damn posterity!

Don't put offerings on my grave,
Nor burn a ceremonial fire.
You'll waste your money. What you give
Is better spent while I am here.

Mixing wine and ash makes mud.
The dead won't drink it for their food.

A boy was setting up a wreath
On his stepmother's tall stone tomb.
He hoped her ashes had become
More kindly; but they caused his death.

The stone fell down and killed the creature.
Stepmothers never change their nature.

Aristo hunted with his sling
The geese to make his poor living.
He stole on them so silently
That they fed and did not fly.
Now he is dead, his sling lies still.
Above his grave, birds dart at will.

God of the Sea, Sodamus the Cretan,
Loved your nets and lived on your wave.
He outdid all in his trade as a fisherman,
But storms do not choose which men they save.

We pray not to sail, Theogenes,
After your death on Libyan seas,
When countless cranes dropped as a cloud
To load your ship to be your shroud.

Much disease on me attended,
While my meals and drinks were few;
But at last my long life ended –
So goddam all of you!

My murderer buried me and hid his crime:
But since he handed me this tomb of mine,
I wish him the same kindness in due time.

Dionysius of Tarsus,
Here's where I rot,
Sixty and unmarried.
God, had my father not!

VARIOUS

On an Unknown Bath

If you want your wife, bathe here,
And brighter you will be to her.
But if lust drives you to a whore,
She will pay for what you paid for.

On a Bath in Byzantium

True the tale of the lotus-eater.
If a man shall once bathe here,
He shall forget country and parents dear.

On an Earthquake

The dead once left the city alive,
Now the living bear the city to her grave.

On the Lost Book of Marcus

Should you wish to conquer care,
Unroll and read this blessed book.
In its pages you will look
On a wealth of learning there.
Things that will be, things that are,
Things that were, all tell the joke –
Joy and pain mean less than smoke.

To a Magistrate

In the cup, mix mild and stern.
For the bee has buzz and sting.
Horse needs whip for its breaking.
Pigs need canes to make them learn.

On an Unworthy Magistrate

Your rise was not the will of Chance.
It's a proof of her omnipotence
That men as low as you advance.

On the Water of Hierapolis

If some one suicidal is
And hates the rope, let him try this –
Drink cold water from Hierapolis.

On a Goat that Suckled a Wolf

Willy-nilly, at my teat,
A wolf-cub sucks all it can eat.
This is my shepherd's idiocy.
The cub, once given suck by me,
Will turn to tear my flesh and blood.
Nature knows no gratitude.

ON STATUES

On the Armed Statue of Aphrodite in Sparta

The goddess of Wisdom saw Love bearing arms.
'Shall we go and be judged so?' she said.
Love smiled: 'Do I need to armour my charms?
What can I not conquer when now I win naked?'

On the Colossus of Rhodes

High as their goal, the Sun, the Dorian men
Of Rhodes rear their colossus to the skies.
Still the bronze tides of battle. Swelling then,
All Rhodes is white with spoil of enemies.
Freedom was chained on distant lands and seas;
The Dorians cut her chains and woke her sleep.
The many sons of the sons of Hercules
Are born to be masters of the earth and deep.

On the Statue of Constantius the Charioteer in the Hippodrome of Byzantium

Awake, Constantius! Why sleep
Your brazen sleep, when the crowd cheers
To see your team and the charioteers
Without you to guide, like orphans, weep?

On a Statue of Justice

'Justice, you look angry. Why?'
'The thief, who set me here on high,
Had not a thing to do with me.'

LEONIDAS

On Myron's Famous Bronze Statue of a Heifer

Myron lied: he did not mould me.
From the herd, he drove me boldly
And fixed me on this stone to hold me.

JULIANUS, PREFECT OF EGYPT

On Myron's Famous Bronze Statue of a Heifer

Look on Myron's statue and confess:
'Art lives, or Nature is lifeless.'

ANONYMOUS

On a Statue of Nemesis

Nemesis holds a bridle and a rule,
The first to curb the gossip of the fool,
The second as the overmighty's school.

On a Statue of Niobe

The gods made a stone of my living flesh.
This stone of Praxiteles makes me live afresh.

On Praxiteles' Statue of Aphrodite

In Cnidus, the goddess of Love looked and said:
'Where did Praxiteles see me naked?'

On a Statue of a Satyr

Either art caught a satyr in the metal once,
Or a satyr slipped into the molten bronze.

On the Statue of Zeus at Olympia

Phidias, either God dropped by
To see you, or you saw Him on high.

ENIGMAS, ORACLES, AND RIDDLES

Enigma

Speechless, you shall speak my name.
Must you speak? Why then again
In speaking you shall say the same.

Answer: Silence.

A Riddle

I am black, my father white.
I have no wings, yet fly sky-high.
Tears follow me when I go by.
The air and I at birth unite.

Answer: Smoke.

On a Mirror

Look at me, and I look at you.
I have no eyes, yet you have two.
My lips will speak without a voice,
While yours are making all the noise.

An Oracle of the Pythia

Even the gods may not evade
Their fate once it is made.

An Oracle given by Serapis

Stranger, the gods do you no wrong.
Wrong was your father to have a son.

EPIGRAMS
ON THE
FAMOUS DEAD

ANONYMOUS

My rhyming verses on these pages
Tell the words of the seven sages.
Cleobulus of Lindus
Said, *Measure will befriend us.*
Chilon of Lacaedemon
Said, *Know yourself,* and was done,
While Corinth's Periander
Advised us, *Master anger.*
Pittacus of Mytilene
Found *Nothing too much* was seemly,
Yet Athenian Solon's giving
Was *Look to the end of living.*
Priene heard her Bias
Say, *Most men are thieves and liars,*
While Thales' words still greet us,
Don't be sure, from Miletus.

LEONTIUS SCHOLASTICUS

Ajax lies in Troy. His thousand victories
Reproach his friends and praise his enemies.

ADDAEUS

If you would sing Alexander of Macedon,
Sing that both continents are his tomb.

ANONYMOUS

Anacreon lies here. O passerby,
Pour wine on this wine-lover. I am dry.

ANTIPATER OF SIDON

Let the four-leaved ivy spread
Where Anacreon may lie,
Let flowers raise their purple head,
Let milk foam to the sky,
Let wine spill from his ashy bed
To show joy cannot die,
To show delight can touch the dead –
Or must it pass them by?

ANONYMOUS

What Clytaemnestra might have said when
Orestes was on the Point of Killing her

Belly or breast, which will you stick me through?
The belly bore you, the breasts fed you.

Democritus once laughed and said:
'Laughter is all.' Now he is dead,
He too can see the reason why
We laugh to see his wisdom die.

ANTIPATER

Here lies the Dog, Diogenes,
Who once gave up the life of ease.
One cloak, one staff, one wallet made
Him self-sufficient in his trade.

Turn, fools! In hell as in Sinope,
Mean men are still his enemy.

ANTIPHILUS OF BYZANTIUM

On Diogenes

The wise Dog thought five things enough
For life: a wallet, and watered barley-dough,
A cloak, a staff to hold him up,
Also an earthenware drinking-cup.
Yet when he saw a countryman
Drink from the hollow of his palm,
He knew he had too much and said:
'Why do I carry a cup instead?'

DIOGENES LAERTIUS

'Remember my words, and adieu,'
Epicurus says to his friends.
He takes a warm bath, and wine too,
Then a cup of cold death, and ends.

ANONYMOUS

All Greece is your tomb, O Euripides.
Your song never dies in the Peloponnese.

PHILEMON

If the dead could really see whom they please,
I'd hang myself to see Euripides.

ACERATUS GRAMMATICUS

Hector, you were Homer's joy.
When the god-built walls of Troy
Saw you fall, then Homer's will
With the Iliad lay still.

ANONYMOUS

I am Heraclitus. I despise
The pack of the illiterate.
My work was not to popularize,
But to teach few. For I equate
One man to thirty thousand, and the mass,
Even in Hades, is as grass.

ANTIPATER OF SIDON

Stranger, the sea beats on the land
That lies on Homer. By his tongue,
Heroes are brave, the gods command,
A second sun is lit among
The Greeks, the Muses are enthralled.
His voice is young in all the world.

ANONYMOUS

Nature bore Homer with mighty labour,
And sank back too tired to bear such another.

In what country was Homer born?
All cities claim him as their own.
His origins remain unknown.

For the Muses hide in a secret place,
Immortal as the gods, his land and race.

Another anonymous epigram states that seven cities claimed the birth of Homer: Argos, Athens, Chios, Colophon, Cyme, Pylos, and Smyrna. Yet other epigrams mention the claims of Cyprus, Egypt, Ios, Ithaca, Mycenae, Salamis, and Thessaly.

HOMER
(or Cleobulus of Lindus)

As long as the waters flow,
And leaves on tall cedars grow,
Here I lie, a maid of brass,
On Midas' tomb. To all who pass,
I tell his tale and burial,
And weep for him my tears of metal.

ANONYMOUS

If the lark laments like the swan,
And the owl rivals the nightingale,
And the cicada by the cuckoo's outdone,
Then I am Palladius' equal.

On Pompey the Great

Many temples were built for him.
When he died, he had no stone.

ANTIPATER

I am small, the tomb of Priam the great.
His foes have built me so, to shame his state.

ANONYMOUS

Protagoras' sharp arrow does no harm.
For wisdom cannot wound; it is a balm.

JULIANUS, PREFECT OF EGYPT

On Pyrrho, the Sceptic Philosopher

'Are you dead, Pyrrho?' 'That I doubt.'
'You doubt, even when your life's put out?'
'I doubt.' 'The tomb puts doubt to rout.'

XENOPHANES

They say Pythagoras passed by
A beaten dog, and, pitying,
Said: 'Stop your blows. His soul within
Is a friend's soul. I heard him cry.'

PINYTUS

Sappho lies here. Her bones are dumb.
But her wrought words outcry the tomb.

THE EPITAPH OF SARDANAPALUS

Knowing you were born to die,
Take your fill of food and cheer.
No joy is where dead men lie.
I was king of Nineveh,
And now am powder. What I ate,
I have, and what I learnt of love;
But I have left my rich estate.
Learn from me and wisely live.

ANONYMOUS

On Sardanapalus

All I ate and drank I have,
And the joys I learnt from Love;
But the things which riches gave,
Those I have to leave above.

ANTIPATER OF THESSALONICA

So great a man in so little earth?
He who sees you, Socrates,
Must blame Greek fools who put to death
The best of us. They knew no mercies,
Nor shame for what they did then.
Athenians are like that often.

SIMIAS

On the tomb of Sophocles,
Let ivy gently grow,
Let roses bloom among green leaves,
Let vines downdropping go,
Heavy with grapes, to shade the grave
Of words both wise and fair
That Grace and Muse together gave
To the sweet singer there.

ANONYMOUS

The tomb is small of Thales here,
But the fame of this astronomer
Reaches to the farthest star.

DIODORUS

A stranger lies in a strange land.
It is Themistocles, whose hand
Saved Athens from the Medes. This stone
Magnesia raised to him alone.

Envy won the victory.
A brave man's deeds are less than she.

ANONYMOUS

*Tiberius and Nero are said to have quoted these
lines often*

When I am dead, mix earth with fire.
Who cares? I have all I desire.

PTOLEMY

On Timon the Misanthrope

Ignore my name and my country.
You see my tomb. I hope you die.

CALLIMACHUS

On Timon the Misanthrope

'Dead Timon, which is worse, darkness or light?'
'Darkness: in Hell, more men offend my sight.'

CHRISTIAN
EPIGRAMS

ANONYMOUS

The blind from birth saw Christ arise,
For His grace has a sea of eyes.

Queen of Heaven, with your child
On your breast, the Son of God,
Make Him merciful and mild,
Although the angels fear His rod.

Guard Him, keep Him safe from harm,
For the whole world rocks upon your arm.

A manger in Heaven, yes, greater than Heaven.
A heaven on earth is through a child given.

Christ the Lord went down to Hell,
Took away each dead man's soul,
Left Hell as empty as a well.

On the Pillar of Holy Daniel
by the Bosphorus

Half in earth and half in heaven,
On a pillar stands a man,
The picking winds he does not fear,
His hunger is ambrosia,
His thirst is wine. He is never done
With tale of Virgin and her Son.